ON THE SHOULDERS
OF LEADERS

- A Leadership Pocket Guide

In the end, leadership is all about people.

JAMES FANTAUZZO, PH.D.

ARPress
ILLUMINATING IDEAS,
EMPOWERING VOICES

ARPress
45 Dan Road Suite 5
Canton MA 02021
Hotline: 1(888) 821-0229
Fax: 1(508) 545-7580

Ordering Information:
Quantity sales. Special discounts are available on quantity purchases by corporations, associations, and others. For details, contact the publisher at the address above.

Printed in the United States of America.

ISBN-13:   Softcover   979-8-89330-954-6
            eBook   979-8-89330-953-9

Library of Congress Control Number: 2024902543

About the Author

Dr. James Fantauzzo, President of Creative Training Solutions, is one of America's most dynamic Management Consultants and Human Resources experts.

For the past twenty-five years Dr. Fantauzzo has provided professional services for the health care, manufacturing, and hospitality industries, in addition to academia. As a consultant, trainer, speaker, and author, Dr. Fantauzzo has helped companies overcome organizational performance concerns in areas related to training and development, team building, employee relations, customer service, and leadership. Jim has received national recognition as a speaker and presenter of seminars and workshops. He has earned the reputation of helping companies solve their employee organizational concerns. He is also a member of the Christian Coaches Network and the National Speakers Association.

In addition to serving various industries, he has taught at the undergraduate and post-graduate levels for several universities, including Barry University and Alfred University for many years. Dr. Fantauzzo continues to devote his time and energy to assisting organizations and their people to improve their leadership capabilities.

Acknowledgements

I dedicate this book to the many individuals, peers, teachers, and family and friends who have influenced my writing development. I am indebted to the many fine people I have had the privilege of working with and serving. So much of my knowledge came from research, clients, teaching, and colleagues.

I also want to thank Lara Wright for her technical computer competence, support, and overall knowledge.

My goal is to provide the business world with a resource of high utility, realism, and value.

With special thanks to my wife, Linda, and our children; Tim, Todd, and Stacey—they helped me to continue dreaming. Your love, joy, and happiness has brought a sense of accomplishment to my life.

I want to give special thanks to all the men and women who have opened their hearts and shared their leadership stories with me. Your commitment to leadership and people makes the business world a better place.

Testimonials

I just wanted to express my sincere appreciation for the dedication that you have shown to the educational program here at Heritage Christian Home. Your sincerity and wisdom is felt immediately by the participants. You speak from the heart with passion and commitment and that is irreplaceable.

Marisa E. Geitner, Organizational Development
Heritage Christian Home

We thank you very much for speaking at the FLAILM Annual Educational Conference. I have received very positive responses and the recommendation that you be asked back.

James R. Stine, Conference Co-Chairman
Tingue, Brown & Co.

I would like to thank you for the excellent training, *The Art of Exceeding Customer Expectations in Healthcare.* The participants found the training to be interesting, informative and very useful for their performance as marketing and customer service executives.

Nanette M. Dumont, Executive Assistant
Triple-S, Inc. Blue Cross and Blue Shield of Puerto Rico

I find Jim to be extremely compassionate, responsive and always professional in his facilitation. Jim's materials are concise and carefully prepared. He holds his audience's attention and the evaluations we receive are always favorable and extremely complimentary of Jim's style of delivery.

Saralie R. Foote, Manager, Training
Industrial Management Council

Thank you! Your presentation on *Improving Teamwork: Voyage to Excellence* at our chapter meeting of IAAP was wonderful. We have heard nothing but positive feedback since our meeting.

Erika J. Kemblowski, CPS, Vice-President
Flower City Chapter IAAP

Dr. James Fantauzzo serves as a Human Resources Consultant to Optical Gaging Productions, Inc. Jim has modernized and streamlined our staffing selection process, personnel training, and development, appraisal, and feedback system by providing specific recommendations on how to improve each area of the work environment.

His management style and leadership efforts have generated far-reaching improvements in our corporate culture.

Our managers have a higher level of awareness and effectiveness regarding the human resources that they control. Jim's recommendations resulted in significant cost savings to the corporation.

We now have a program that has reduced our cost of hiring. We have a system that co-ordinates manpower needs and the staff available, taking greater advantage of our ability to promote from within the corporations.

Edward T. Polidor, President
Optical Gaging Products, Inc.

Dear Dr. Fantauzzo,

I wanted to take this opportunity to thank you for the excellent presentation you did for our October 15, 1997, Western New York Educational Conference. The entire group of attendees very well received the two seminars.

It was also very much appreciated at how you tailored these two areas specifically to not only to the health care industry, but also specifically to individuals in our profession. This gave greater meaning, and I believe greater participation, to our Conference. I look forward to the possibility of having you again in the future.

Terry Cole, Conference Chairman
The McGuire Group

Dear Dr. Fantauzzo,

I am writing to thank you again for your generous gesture in providing our staff with the wonderful leadership training on May 2, 2003. We are all trying to put the valuable information to work. I personally have begun looking at our evaluation and feedback policies and have been considering some of your suggestions. I have also decided to use "art mart" at our next directors' meeting on May 30. It was my favorite part of the training. Thank you again.

Sheila Young, S.A.I.L. Coordinator
Kids' Harbor Preschool & Child Care

Dear Dr. Fantauzzo,

First, I would like to compliment you on a fine presentation at the Customer Satisfaction Conference in Washington, D.C., last month. Not only was your presentation content meaningful but your treatment of adult learning theory was impeccable.

Dr. Fantauzzo, it was refreshing to see someone so confident in their own professional station to allow others, such as myself, to offer our experience without cutting us off or diminishing the effect of your wonderful presentation. Your ability to think on your feet and maintain a significant presence in the room was simply remarkable.

Michael P. Grinnals, Director of Education & Training,
Thompson Health

Dear Dr. Fantauzzo,

On behalf of the staff at Melles Griot Optical Systems, I would like to take this opportunity to thank you for the excellent training you have provided. The participants found the weekly training sessions to be well planned, informative, and an asset to their professional careers. The skills learned during the training sessions could be instantly put to use with the day-to-day issues faced among the participants. It was apparent that a great deal of preparation went into this customized training program. Upon completion of this five-week program, the participants gained the knowledge and confidence needed to improve their skills.

Deborah Gsellmeier, Human Resources Manager
Melles Griot Optical Systems

Dear Dr. Fantauzzo:

On behalf of all the members of the Employees Communication Council, we would like to express our gratitude for all you have done for our hospital.

Although you were here for such a short time, your charisma and dynamic personality has resulted in much-needed advances toward better communication between management and employees, thus moving our institution in a positive direction.

The officers would particularly like to thank you for the extra time you gave to us. Your suggestions and guidance were appreciated.

Tillie Fulton, RN, Chairperson
Joe Lowe, Vice Chairperson
Pat Quattrone, Secretary
Olean General Hospital

Dear Dr. Bottenberg,

As a recent graduate of Warren National University's doctoral program in Health Administration, I'd like to take a moment to share my gratitude and appreciation for Dr. Fantauzzo, who was my dissertation advisor. Dr. Fantauzzo's knowledge, patient guidance, and leadership are outstanding. Distance learning can have its challenges for some students, but dedicated teachers like Dr. Fantauzzo make all the difference.

If it were not for Dr. Fantauzzo, I might not have finished my degree. For the past seven years I have had chronic Hodgkin's Lymphoma, which requires that I periodically take chemotherapy to shrink tumors when they become too big. During the last two months of my dissertation a tumor was found behind my heart and I had to begin weekly chemotherapy. I wasn't sure if I had the physical or mental strength to continue my degree and was on the verge of giving up. Dr. Fantauzzo would not let me give up. He was the rainbow in a state of chaos. He believed in me, and his belief gave me the strength to believe in myself and continue onward. Dr. Fantauzzo has become a trusted friend and mentor. I feel blessed to have had such an incredible teacher.

Dr. Michelle Miller, PhD Graduate
Warren National University

Dr. Fantauzzo has a very impressive background and experience in the areas of human resources, management, business, leadership development, motivational speaking, and he uses all of this marvelous background in the classroom.

During two different terms in the years 2000 and 2007, Dr. Fantauzzo taught

Administration 646, Human Resource Administration on the undergraduate level, at Barry University's School of Adult and Continuing Education (ACE), on the Treasure Coast. On their course evaluation forms, the students said that they found their instructor to be very knowledgeable of the subject area, and an excellent source of information. There was general agreement that the course was well taught, and that Dr. Fantauzzo really cared about his students. Several mentioned that they would definitely take another course from this instructor should the opportunity present itself.

I personally observed Dr. Fantauzzo in the ACE classroom and found him to be well prepared, and there was good interaction and rapport between instructor and students. It was obvious that Jim loved being in the classroom, helping students to acquire new knowledge that would be helpful to them on both professional and personal levels. We hope to schedule Dr. Fantauzzo for another class in the near future.

Sister Grace Flowers, OP
Associate Director and Student Advisor
Barry University, School of Adult and Continuing Education

I would like to offer this letter of recommendation for Dr. James Fantauzzo. Dr. Fantauzzo has been a faculty member in the School of Business at Warner Southern for the past several years. He has taught a number of different courses at the undergraduate and graduate levels on management and leadership. Dr. Fantauzzo's students have always rated him as one of their best professors. During his time here, he has been a contributing member of the faculty and the school.

In addition to his abilities as a faculty member, I have found him to be of the highest character.

William M. Rigel,

PhD Executive Vice President and Chief Academic Officer

Warner Southern University

Foreword

In putting together *On The Shoulders of Leaders* it was my goal and purpose to offer practical daily leadership wisdom, advice, and inspiration to meet the many challenges in our daily work lives.

If you are a supervisor, manager, director, vice-president, president, trainer, consultant, coach, student, or military leader, then by design, this book was written for you.

The ideas, research, and preparation of this book required patience, careful thought and analysis, and continuous editing. Perhaps one of the most important factors was the belief that this book would provide realistic and useful information to help all managers—current and future—to understand the importance of proactive and effective leadership.

The approaches described here are related to business strategies and proven ideas that have resulted from my experience as a management consultant, speaker, trainer, and as a Corporate Human Resource professional in the real world of business.

In the final analysis, the purpose of leadership is to demonstrate commitment to the success of the people being led, to earn their trust, and to treat them with respect. As a leader, your success starts with theirs.

I am pleased that you are reading *On The Shoulders of Leaders*. I expect that many of you will continue to use this book through the years. You will want to refer to certain sections again and again to review the information relating to the various leadership issues you are dealing with at various times in your career.

I am available to assist organizations in health care, manufacturing, hospitality, and academia. I devote my time and energy to helping organizations and people to improve their leadership capabilities.

The best way to reach me is by e-mail: cts7349@msn.com or through my website: www.creativetrainingsolutions.net. I hope that you will consider staying in touch with me to let me know what has worked for you as a leader.

Introduction

Prescription for Leadership: The Purpose of Driven Leadership

*O*n the Shoulders of Leaders (a.k.a. *Leadership Pocket Guide*) is a book for leaders who aspire to lead and who want to make positive changes within the organization.

The business need for proactive leadership in all segments of business is critically important for today and tomorrow. The primary purpose of this Pocket Guide is to assist managers at all levels to fully utilize those skills necessary to run their businesses each and every day.

A lack of leadership skills and experience in a manager may have a negative impact on the employees are under his or her supervision. In writing the Leadership Pocket Guide, I intended to make it an easy-to-use, realistic reference that will assist each manager in his or her administrative and operational responsibilities.

In the real world of business, managers are extremely busy professionals. The *Leadership Pocket Guide* will assist them in accomplishing their day-to-day responsibilities effectively, and in a timely fashion. In the business world, there is a significant need for proactive leadership at all levels within organizations. Today, many management people do not have the necessary training to be effective leaders. Talent is helpful in a leadership role; however, commitment, credibility, tenacity, and continuous training are also necessary for effectiveness. The purpose of leadership is to take responsibility for the organization and to make the Vision and Mission Statements a reality in order remain competitive and to grow the business for the future.

The *Leadership Pocket Guide* has been prepared for those individuals who have a desire to improve their leadership skills, and who have a desire to make a difference through their daily contribution as managers. The *Leadership Pocket Guide* will define how to practice sound leadership concepts. Acquiring knowledge is important, but how the concepts are used is even more important.

What this *Leadership Pocket Guide* will do for you

This Pocket Guide lists and describes the key components that will help managers to perform more efficiently in meeting and exceeding the goals of their organizations.

The simple steps that I have set down here are based on tested and proven approaches to employee management and operational topics and issues, and the steps and actions that will work effectively.

The fact that you are reading this Guide indicates that you may be looking for useful tools that will improve your individual performance and your overall contribution to your organization.

The Pocket Guide reference covers ways to achieve success when administering various policies and procedures or trying to resolve operational or employee problems.

Let's begin the journey that will lead you to improved per-formance, significant accomplishment, and more success for you and your team.

Table of Contents

Chapter 1

Organizational Goals

STRATEGIC UNDERPINNINGS

Many larger organizations have written Vision and Mission Statements as an important strategic way in which to run their businesses.

The Vision and Mission Statement are linked to the culture, the strategic planning process, the customer base, and how the organization is planning to run the business, both near-term and long-term.

The Annual Operating Plan (AOP) is defined as a strategic plan for the next twelve-month period. The longer-term strategic plan defines the goals over the coming three-year period.

The one-year strategic plan is prepared using a process in which all of the senior managers prepare their business plans for review and submission into the strategic plan. The size and structure of the organization will determine which members of senior management will make submissions into the annual operating plan and the long-term strategic plan. Typically, these submissions include goals for Marketing, Finance, Manufacturing, Research and Development, International Business, Human Resources, and Engineering.

After these plans are submitted, reviewed, and finalized, they become the final business plan for the year. During the year, members of senior management may be required to give quarterly reports. This is to inform and update the entire senior management team about the progress and the status of each department. Based upon this report, adjustments may be made to ensure that the goals of each department will be met.

It is important to note that all of the strategic plans are submitted to the president, general manager, or the corporate office for review and approval. Once again, the review and approval process will be dependent upon the culture and policies of each organization. In recent years, many businesses have been forced to redefine themselves in an effort to build services and financial operations. They must also be masters of detail with regard to their goals and strategies for success.

Chapter 2

Building Trust-Relationships: The Voice of Leadership

CULTIVATING PEOPLE RESOURCES

Building good organizational relationships among their employees should be an important goal in all business cultures. If senior management stresses the importance of this practice throughout the organization, and makes this a part of the Vision and Mission Statements, this renewed positive behavior will result in higher quality and more credible communication. This behavior among managers will reflect the beliefs, values, and actions of senior management. Managing the environment in this manner, a stronger leadership will emerge and become more visible to the employees within the organization. When an organization harnesses the power of proactive leadership the following changes will become visible and measurable:

- Teams will be stronger.
- The organization's vision and mission goals will be met.
- Morale will be improved.
- There will be more cooperation among managers and employees of various departments.

- Customer service will be improved.
- Financial goals will be met or exceeded.
- Employee turnover may be reduced.
- A win-win environment will become more evident within the organization.
- Employees' positive beliefs, attitudes, and behaviors will be established as norms.

For any environment to function smoothly, a high level of trust is needed between the leaders and teams of employees within each department.

Leadership through Partnership

So much of our identity comes from our relationships. How we as leaders relate to others, and how they relate to us, teaches us important things about ourselves. For people to work effectively together, we must admit to ourselves that we need each other. Relationships will take on a much deeper meaning when people in business accept this behavioral fact.

Leadership through partnership involves building teams throughout the organization, department by department. This may require a paradigm shift throughout the organization. This can only be accomplished by each manager displaying proactive leadership, commitment, and thorough, purposeful, and high-quality communication. This paradigm shift may also require continuous auditing and accountability to ensure it is making progress.

The purposes for cultivating the seeds of leadership include:

- High employee morale
- Meaningful and attainable goals
- Effective communication
- Continuous employee training based upon a Needs Assessment Instrument
- Excellent team dynamics (both Inter and Intra)

- Regularly scheduled State-of-the-business meetings facilitated by senior management
- Meaningful employee rewards system
- Effective safety program
- Excellent product or service
- Profitability objectives
- Continuous research and development
- Internal employee promotion system
- Stress reduction training programs
- Employee performance review system
- Employee assistance resource program

Talent is very helpful in leadership, but courage is also necessary.

All leaders should display patience when leading to include a situational leadership approach in an effort to address and resolve various problems or concerns within the organization.

Chapter 3

Recruiting Employees

When organizations need to implement a recruitment plan, they normally use the services of a human resources department. Quite often, a human resources department includes an employment manager function.

The employment manager has the responsibility to use cost effective recruitment methods to fill openings quickly. The methods of recruitment are very dependent upon the number of openings that the organization currently has within each department. In order to run the business efficiently, all openings should be staffed as quickly as possible. Additionally, the various openings may be categorized between hourly positions and professional positions.

Filling all of the openings as quickly as possible is dependent upon the Employment Manager using various recruitment methods to attract qualified candidates. The methods of recruitment include: field recruiting, college recruiting, employee referral, Advertising, Employment Agency, Online Recruiting, Chamber of Commerce Bulletin Boards, and holding an open house or job fair. These recruiting methods have stood the test of time, and can be useful and effective.

Most organizations have an annual recruiting budget. The various financial considerations that become part of the budget preparation for each year is typically based upon the experience of the previous year in employee turnover.

Two key points to know are the following: a) It is extremely important that the individuals involved in the recruiting process be trained and gain experience conducting interviews; b) Proper placement of new hires is critically important. Having the right people in the right positions at the right time to achieve organizational objectives is critical.

In some cases, it may be faster and more cost effective to conduct screening interviews by telephone prior to inviting candidates for in-person meetings. This initial assessment process may help you determine that the candidate may not have the qualifications needed to fill the position. This may save time and money for the organization.

Chapter 4

The Employment Interview

It is critically important to hire the right people at the right time to run the business and meet organizational objectives. When a position within the organization becomes vacant, the recruiting process will begin to find a number of qualified candidates with whom to begin the interview process. If a human resources department exists within the organization, the recruiting people will take the lead, pre-screening candidates before the hiring department interviews them.

After the candidates are selected and scheduled for an interview, they come into the human resources department or the hiring department to complete the employment application form. This process also includes completing an application online as may be requested by the organization. This provides the necessary information for the interviewers to assess whether the candidate has the necessary background to fill the open position.

To be prepared for the scheduled interviews, the employment application and a resume should be reviewed. This kind of preparation is required in order to conduct a professional and legal interview. The interviewer could retrieve information associated with a legal interview versus a non-legal interview by going online to research additional information. This will allow the interviewer to be ready to ask focused, relevant, and legal questions.

When the candidate arrives at the scheduled date and time, he or she should be treated as a guest. This will help ensure that the individual leaves the interview with a positive impression of the interviewer and the organization. There have many instances in which a candidate is treated poorly and unprofessionally because the interviewer wasn't prepared or trained on how to conduct a professional interview. When this happens, the candidate may leave with a very negative impression of the interviewer and the organization.

Please refer to pages 133, 134 and 135 for visuals illustrating proper interview processes.

Chapter 5
Internal Promotions

Today, a high percentage of organizations have internal promotion policies and systems that enable existing employees to get promoted into positions of greater responsibility. The Internal Promotion Policy is typically administered by a member of the Human Resources department and the hiring manager. The process usually begins by interviewing those employees who have applied to be considered for the open position. The initial screening is done by a member of the Human Resources Department. Once this is completed, those employees who have the requisite skills would be scheduled to be interviewed by the hiring manager.

This policy is clearly positive for employees. It is good for morale, it provides internal growth of responsibilities and pay, and it is cost effective for the company.

Chapter 6

Management, Manpower, Succession Planning

THE ADMINISTRATIVE PROCESS

The Succession Planning Process is a strategic system that considers the manpower planning needs of an organization, both near-term and long-term. This administrative process requires the involvement of the chief executive officer (CEO) or a general manager—essentially someone who is responsible for a division, company, a hospital, or a corporation—to plan for anticipated vacancies.

This is a systematic staffing process that requires a great deal of analysis and planning to select the right candidate/employee to fill this vacancy. The key employees involved in the administrative process should be the senior Human Resources officer, who could be a corporate director, divisional director, company manager, or director. This, of course, depends upon how the organization's reporting relationships are structured.

This process typically takes place on an annual basis and its goal is to plan for anticipated vacancies for the near-term and long-term. The near-term could be defined as "Annual Operating Procedure," or a three to five-year period. In many cases, depending upon the various operating strategies the organization has in place, this process could be integrated into the organization's business plans. This internal recruiting and placement program is structured to fill vacancies with an effective and professional internal placement procedure.

The key steps involved in the process are to analyze the existing members of senior management who report to the president, general manager, hospital administrator, and so on, to determine the following:

- Who will be retiring in the near future?
- If this person is promoted to another division within the corporation or company, who would be ready to take his or her place?
- What if this person decides to resign for better career opportunities?

If a senior management position remains open for any period of time, some portion of the business will not be accomplished. This could have far reaching and negative impacts on the business.

Once it is agreed that a Succession Planning Strategy for internally promoted employees should be implemented, along with all the various administrative steps, the following should be included in the program:

Design and complete assessment forms to document the profiles of the managers who could be considered for promotion. Include:

- Hire date
- Current salary
- Education
- Performance reviews

Upon reviewing all of the profile data of each employee, the human resources executive and senior management team makes a decision regarding who is promotable or not. The decision-making process is the responsibility of senior management members. They conduct a review and audit of all promotable employees.

This kind of analysis requires a very careful and thorough review by a trained and objective assessor. This individual is usually the senior Human Resources officer from the corporate office, the division, or the company.

After the assessments are completed in writing, this information becomes confidential, and is not discussed with the candidate employees.

Once this process begins, it should be continued and maintained—there are many benefits to this type of program.

If successors cannot be identified within the organization, then outside recruiting would begin as soon as possible.

For internal candidates who aren't yet ready for promotion, the process requires supporting actions needed to ensure that they gain the skills needed for promotion. This list may include going back to school, attending seminars, or both. This is part of the organization's commitment to preparing high-potential successors.

There are times when the employee is informed that he or she is a "high potential" candidate, and there may be situations when the employee shouldn't be told. These are decisions that are made by the senior Human Resources officer and the person in charge of running the business—the President, General Manager, or other designated person.

Unlocking the talent of high potential employees in the organization starts with a commitment to do so—the organization's commitment and the employee's commitment. For one to access one's true hidden talents one must be given the opportunity and training needed in order to find one's true authenticity in which to be promoted into greater responsibility. This can only be accomplished when the organization opens the door through commitment and leadership.

Running the business using this kind of Succession Planning has a positive effect on morale, motivation, productivity, team cohesiveness, turnover, and is a cost-effective way to improve recruiting.

Management, Manpower, Succession Planning
Summary

These administrative processes are linked to near-term and long-term planning of the manpower needed to run the business efficiently with qualified employees. It is a process that involves careful and professional assessment of those professional employees who have been identified as high potentials for promotion. The high potential employees are individuals who have exhibited outstanding performance in their current positions and will soon be ready to be promoted into positions of greater responsibilities.

This kind of planning is needed for near and long-term planning to fill positions that may be vacated as a result of employees retiring or resigning, or leaving for other reasons. The near-term and long-term timelines may range from one year to five years. This will help keep the administrative process current and up to date.

Typically, the Human Resources Department and select members of senior management are involved in this planning process. Additionally, the Succession Planning Process is linked to the organization's near-term and long-term strategic goals.

Chapter 7

Orientation and Training for New Hires

When a new hire enters the organization, it is critically important that the new employee be thoroughly oriented and trained to ensure that he or she becomes productive and successful.

It is important, practical, and logical to provide orientation and training for *all* new hires. Scheduling training soon after hiring will help to ensure that new hires have the knowledge they need to feel comfortable, and to begin to contribute to the organization. These are the resources they will need to ensure they won't have a false start in their new position. To amplify upon the definition of the term false start would mean the employee would display a limited understanding and performance within their current role.

1. It is important for organizations to provide a New Hire Orientation and Training for newly hired employees for the following reasons:

A. It will lay the foundation for the new employee's career and increase their confidence so that they adapt quickly to the new position.

B. It will introduce them to the company, its policies, their coworkers, the company culture, and their job description.

The areas of orientation and training should include the following:

- Introduction to the Vision and Mission Statements (if available)
- Overview of the workplace culture
- Introduction to the employee handbook
- Overview of the services and products offered by the organization
- Company policies and procedures
- Overview of employee benefits offered by the company
- Information about the customers—who are they?

Providing this kind of training and orientation for all new hires establishes an important knowledge base for them.

Chapter 8

Organizational Development Training

The training and development, or Human Resource development, has grown at a tremendous rate for many years and continues to grow rapidly. This growth has been seen in all major organizations of all types, nationally and internationally, because it makes sense to train and retrain employees at all levels within the organization. A well-planned training program will give employees a greater sense of self-worth, increase productivity, create a more positive attitude, and increase employees' self-esteem.

The biggest block to performing ongoing training may be affordability, if financial goals are not being met. If an organization meets the needs of the employees through skills training and cultural information, the employees will meet the needs and goals of the organization.

When designing and planning an employee training program, there are a number of components that need to be discussed prior to implementation. The following ideas should be considered prior to the finalization of a schedule: In many organizations, the training of employees is often mentioned in the organization's Mission Statement and Annual Operating Plan.

Once it has been determined that training programs are necessary, definitive training goals should be established. It isn't sufficient to say, "We want to improve the employees' knowledge, skills, attitudes, and behavior." It is important to clarify what is to change, specifically, why the changes are necessary, and by department, if appropriate. Also, when planning a training program, timelines should be established for each training topic. This is important to ensure the training objectives are met and to avoid a false start.

The initial process should include the following:

- What training will be conducted, and where and when
- Who will facilitate the training
- Why the training is important and what the expected outcomes are

Lastly, a letter or email should be sent to all employees introducing the training. The letter should be sent by the most senior manager (general manager, chief executive officer (CEO), president). The contents of the letter should clearly describe the purpose of the required training programs, and the three items mentioned above.

An employee training program can be a significant learning experience, involving adding skills and knowledge, or changing attitudes or behavior. Ideally, a training program will result in a permanent improvement in each employee's job performance.

The outcome of a well-planned training program may be changes in what employees know, the way they perform their work, and their attitude toward their responsibilities and the organization.

U.S. business firms spend billions of dollars each year on training programs to improve employee performance.

Much of the training is done through formal lecture courses and seminars.

Some organizations contract with consulting firms to plan and conduct their training programs. Leadership will play a critical role in the planning and implementation of an organizational training program, and without strong, committed, and proactive leadership throughout the organization, it is difficult for the organization to become a continuous learning environment.

If a learning environment within the organization is to progress, everyone will need to agree on a shared vision with regard to training for all employees. It will be the organization that values continuous learning and strongly believes positives outcomes can be derived from implementation of well-coordinated training programs.

All training and development planned in an organization should, ideally, be cost effective. The benefits to be gained must outweigh the costs of training.

Without a shared vision and the support of the CEO and Human Resources management, the training becomes a waste of time and resources.

In a learning organization, all members take an active role in identifying and addressing performance-related concerns. This will be accomplished by sharing and applying newly-acquired knowledge when and where needed.

The implementation of an employee training program will help the organization to shape its future by embracing a voyage of discovery to improve employee performance and productivity. One of the most important outcomes would be to create openness and trust among co-workers and more respect for each other. Other outcomes of effective training are enthusiastic teams, stronger cohesion between team members, and outstanding performance, and these can be related to the bottom line of the organization.

Thousands of organizations are now engaged in planning and implementing training programs. Training continues to be a powerful tool. It is one of the most important ways in which to translate learning and knowledge into skills and action. Employee training will continue to be the interchange between purposeful information and ideas.

This chapter provides some basics for planning and implementing employee training. Ultimately, training programs will be most effective if senior management utilizes their own observations and knowledge and includes prior performance reviews of their employees to choose and conduct meaningful and relevant training programs.

The following training programs should be considered to increase employee skills and performance.

a. Team-based Performance Measurement
b. Team Building Workshop for Supervisors, Managers, and Senior Management
c. Enhancing and Managing Cultural Diversity
d. The Art of Building and Exceeding Customer Satisfaction
e. A Blueprint for Managing Change in the Organization
f. How to improve Morale and Increase Employee Motivation

Chapter 9

The Employee Performance Review Process

The administration of the Employee Performance Review Process is one of the most important responsibilities a manager has. Employee performance reviews are excellent opportunities for managers to meet with subordinates to discuss in detail their performance. In small and large organizations, every employee should be subject to a periodic performance appraisal. The primary purpose of these appraisals has shifted in recent years. Originally, performance reviews were used to provide guidance to management in selecting employees for promotion or salary increases. Appraisals are now also used for coaching employees to improve their performance. As before, an effective performance-appraisal program also provides management with a rational basis for determining who should be promoted and who should receive salary increases.

The question emerges: Why are such a high percentage of the performance review sessions done so poorly? Listed below are some the reasons why this happens so frequently:

- Lack of management commitment
- Lack of planning
- Lack of an effective administrative system to ensure the process begins on the scheduled date
- Human Resources doesn't provide the leadership and influence necessary

The above information is based upon consulting assignments in healthcare, high-technology, and hospitality industries over the past 25 years. 50% of all performance reviews are typically late.

It is critically important for an organization to ensure that all managers who have this responsibility receive training.

When scheduling and conducting an employee review meeting it is extremely important that the manager is well prepared. The preparation should include a thorough review of the employee's file and past performance, and the meeting with the employee should be scheduled at least a week in advance. Preparation and planning will ensure that the performance review session will be professional, friendly, and without interruption.

When the Employee Performance Review is conducted professionally and effectively the results will be very positive—the employee being reviewed will be made to feel important, and the individual's self-esteem and productivity will increase significantly.

One of the most important responsibilities a leader has is to provide performance feedback to his or her employees.

Chapter 10

Employee Morale is Critically Important

LEADERSHIP CIRCLE OF INFLUENCE

The morale of employees in an organization is extremely important. A question frequently asked by leaders is, "How do we maintain good employee morale on a continuous basis?" This should always be a concern of management team members—they are there to provide proactive leadership to all employees. Some of the questions may be the following:

- How can we measure morale?
- How will low morale affect the motivation of employees?
- Will low morale have an effect on employee turnover?
- Will low morale have an effect on productivity?

To answer these questions completely, senior management must address employees' concerns. Additionally, there is a relationship between low morale, low self-esteem, and motivation. If morale is high, then self-esteem, motivation, and productivity will be significantly higher. So how is this accomplished in a way that is timely and cost effective? There are a number of ways linked to leadership that this can be implemented.

The following information on employee morale is based upon empirical data. If management is sincerely concerned about employee morale, there are steps that can be taken to address this concern. For example:

Supervisors and managers should be trained to be familiar with the topics of leadership, effective communications, how to conduct meetings, motivation theory, how to conduct employee performance reviews, the importance of an open-door policy whereby employees feel comfortable speaking to their supervisor in confidence, and the importance of conducting an employee climate survey.

If these topics are built into the culture, there is a very high probability that morale will be and remain high. The key is to provide training programs that address this important concern on a continuous basis.

A "Climate survey" is also known as an Employee Attitude Survey, which assesses how employees feel about working for the organization. This survey gathers facts and statistics to measure all areas of the working environment. After this information is compiled and reviewed by management, actions are put into place to address any concerns that appear.

The worst thing management can do is to conduct an Employee Attitude Survey and then do nothing to address concerns expressed by the employees. This sends a clear signal that management doesn't actually care what employees think about their work environment, and results in a serious loss of credibility for senior management. It would be very difficult for management to recover from this mistake.

Creating and cultivating a positive work environment will improve employee morale and productivity.

Chapter 11

The Importance of Teamwork

TEAMWORK AND TEAM BUILDING IS A PROCESS OF DISTRIBUTING LEADERSHIP

A team is a responsible group of employees who meet regularly to identify problems related to the organization and who work together openly to solve problems. Problem solving is their highest priority with the goal of achieving the *necessary* results. The effectiveness of an organization is greatly influenced by the quality of cooperation among its groups and its individual members. The team-building techniques described in the Pocket Guide have already been used by many organizations. All employees who participate in team building must be prepared to open their minds to new ideas and experiences. They must have a sincere desire to address issues and to build new relationships. These ideas and methods must be tried and tested repeatedly until the desired outcomes are achieved in order to establish world-class efficiency.

The following lists the characteristics of highly effective teams:

- Team members understand and support the leader's goals.
- The team has a genuine desire to work together in an effort to resolve problems.
- There is visible respect among team members.
- Team members always try to give breath and life to the organization's vision and mission statements.

Communications among team members is aimed at achieving the necessary results to address and resolve organizational operational concerns and problems. The team leader or department manager encourages cooperation and synergy among team members to ensure respect and satisfaction among team members.

Within the team culture, problem-solving techniques are utilized in order to resolve conflict and to complete objectives and goals. Management teams are consistently encouraged to utilize their collective professional knowledge and wisdom to solve problems and plan for the future. Teams frequently plan for the future, and assess the status of the business on a monthly, quarterly, semi-annually, and annual basis. Teamwork that results in consistently excellent performance will have a positive impact on morale and can be measured at the financial bottom line.

The following is a list of what to look for when a team becomes dysfunctional:

- Team members avoid conflict.
- The same problems recur and nothing is accomplished.
- Meeting agendas may not be followed, rendering meetings a waste of time.
- The team leader loses control and various team members dominate the meeting—participation becomes limited to only the dominant few.

- Respect for other team members is noticeably absent.
- A sense of responsibility for others within the team appears to be declining.
- Team members' efforts to create a positive and cooperative environment are reduced.
- Unrelated side conversations take place during team meetings.

Team building is a continuous learning process that involves acting with an open mind, and seeking better solutions for business challenges.

- Hold regular group meetings.
- Do not always depend on the written word alone.
- A leader should be a good teacher and communicator.
- A leader should be a problem-solver.
- A leader must know how to manage time well.
- Leaders must know the importance of providing a vision and mission for the organization.
- Leaders should have a sense of humor.
- A leader know the importance of asking employees for advice and suggestion about how to address problems or improve a process or procedure.
- A leader must be a visible role-model.

Chapter 12

Building Trust

Effective and purpose-driven leadership is not possible without trust. Leaders must earn and maintain the trust of their employees throughout the organization from the senior management team to the first line supervisor. If the management team wants to have any degree of credibility, they must earn and maintain a high degree of trust.

Role modeling is an important component of leadership and trust. Employees hear what their leaders *say*, but they watch and observe what they *do*. This is a simplistic definition of Role Modeling. Based upon empirical data from a number of business segments where there is measurable trust in a department or organization, the motivation among employees will be consistently high. If trust is lacking, the opposite indications will be very visible.

There will always be a percentage of employees in every organization who will do only what is required of them—the very minimum to ensure they retain their job—and no more. This behavior will continue until there is a change of the management style of the department to be more proactive. The symptoms that will most commonly emerge in the team are low morale, attrition, possibly a decrease in the quality of the product or service, and gossip. There is a correlation between high self-esteem among employees and motivation. Conversely, when the self-esteem of individual employees is low, then productivity and motivation will also be low. If the needs of the employees are met, then the needs of the department or organization will be met.

High performance can be accomplished only if there is a culture of trust. Within the definition of "Leadership," managers must make every effort to fulfill their important role as leaders. Senior management, more than all leadership positions, has a responsibility to review the leadership methods to ensure that good practices are being applied proactively and effectively. People aspire to identify with organizations that they can respect.

There is a clear correlation between learning, leading, and trust.

Chapter 13

Conflicts: Costly If Not Addressed

There is a high probability that there will be conflicts among department managers and/or employees within an organization.

The best way to prepare employees with the basics of how to address conflict is through training. When there is conflict, employees become frustrated and uncertain, and relationships become strained or broken.

Productivity suffers, goals are not met, and ultimately customers may become dissatisfied with the product or service. A typical dissatisfied customer may tell eight to ten people about the problem they experienced. On average, it can take ten to fourteen positive service experiences to make up for one bad experience. There can be a loss of customers and revenue; something no organization can afford.

Taking time to train employees on conflict resolution methods is critically important. This process starts with leadership, effective communication, and commitment. Training may be scheduled with a professional facilitator, or it may be conducted by a department manager, either formally or informally.

Where there is an issue or disagreement, employees need to focus on the issue and not point fingers at each other. Redirecting fault will only amplify the issue and will not resolve the problem. If there is commitment to resolving the conflict, then quality communication, positive attitude, fact finding, and a sincere desire to resolve the problem will be necessary. If these components are visible and present in an environment of harmony, and not from behind "departmental fences," the conflict can be resolved to everyone's satisfaction. Resolving conflict requires the leaders to be credible and committed, and to display situational leadership. Sometimes problems or issues are very visible within various departments and should be address and resolved using situational leadership.

Chapter 14

Attitude Is Everything

Webster's Dictionary defines attitude as: "A mental position with regard to a fact or state; a position assumed for a specific purpose; a feeling of emotion toward a fact or state."

Attitude is extremely important for how an employee approaches his or her job on a daily basis. The employee's position in the organization doesn't matter. What does matter is that each employee tries to develop and maintain a positive attitude. A positive attitude can be contagious.

Also important is that the manager of a department or team know each member, and how to keep them focused and motivated. This can only be done if the manager is familiar with the behavioral patterns of each team member. Knowing and understanding each individual and having some insight into each one's personality will allow the leader to resolve any problems within the department. Leaders are defined by their good intentions, good deeds, and results. Keeping the department members motivated, and understanding their needs will result in synergy for the team, ensuring compatibility, and allowing the group to meet or exceed the department's goals.

Proactive leadership needs to be consistent and ongoing to develop people and teams. This involves continuous and high-quality communication every day. Without quality communication, leadership is incomplete.

It is always important to be generous with praise for a job well done.

Chapter 15

Optimizing Communication and Feedback

"Clear communications associated with expectations" is defined as a person sending a message to another individual for the purpose of evoking a response. There is a sender, a receiver, and a message that may be verbal, non-verbal, or behavioral. Full communication is achieved when the receiver understands the full meaning of the message as it was intended by the sender. This must include not only the content, as carried by the words, but also the special meaning that may have influenced the selection of the words used in order for the message to be effective. Communication involves at least two individuals—the sender of information and the receiver of the message. The receiver receives the sender's message and responds to the information, and sends the sender a verbal or nonverbal message to complete the message. This process may include written memos, email messages, verbal communication, and any exchanges that may take place in various meetings.

Effective leadership is the attainment of organizational goals in an effective and efficient manner through planning, organizing, and controlling organizational resources. This cannot be done without purposeful, effective, and continuous communication. One of the most important building blocks for team performance is open communication. All members of the team are encouraged to participate in decision-making discussions. These decisions may involve roles and responsibilities, operating procedures, and other leadership decisions.

Without good communication, proactive leadership will be less effective, and will result in costly waste to the organization.

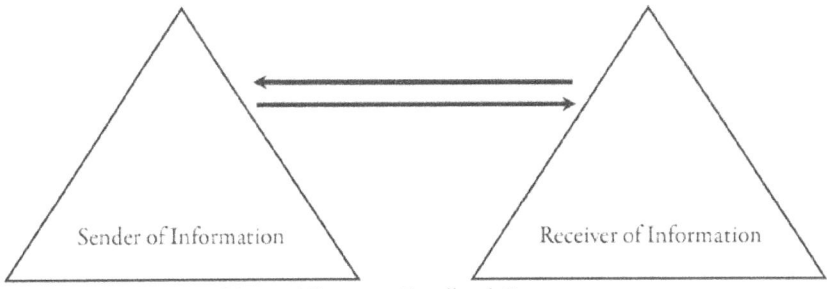

Organizational Leadership Communication Model

Sender of Information

Receiver of Information

Normal Business Feedback Process

- Both parties may need to adjust/revise information in order to ensure understanding.

- Without effective communications, pro-active leadership will be reduced and the results will be costly waste to the organization.

Figure 15.1

Chapter 16

Organizational Change

To survive and succeed, every organization must turn itself into a change agent. The most effective way to manage change successfully is to create the change. This is especially so in large organizational changes involving new technologies, new strategies, e-business, restructuring, mergers, acquisitions, and globalization.

When and where appropriate, individual managers and supervisors should recommend and make changes to improve organizational effectiveness. This is also called "situational leadership."

Examples include improving employee morale, implementing a safety program, introducing quality improvement programs, ways to save the organization money, training for conducting effective and productive meetings, and so on. Providing leadership underpins the organization, and is the role of all individuals who have managerial responsibility. It isn't how smart a leader is that is important. What is important is how leaders use their intelligence relevant to leading and managing change.

Understanding what the organization requires from its leadership team to accomplish ongoing success will always be important. Leaders should not need permission to provide situational leadership when and where needed. Proactive Leadership should always be cultivated and encouraged, rather than a "pushership" style of leadership, or management by fear. This doesn't mean doing away with discipline. If an employee is displaying a pattern of poor performance, or absenteeism, or some other form of unacceptable behavior, discipline should be administered. The Employee Discipline Policy should, ideally, be detailed in the Employee Handbook. Progressive discipline should be applied as fairly as possible.

When management recognizes the need for a change of any kind, the management team should consider how to implement the change for maximum effectiveness. This requires the organized abandonment of things that have been shown to be unsuccessful. In this regard, how the changes will be implemented is extremely important. All realistic options should be considered. For example, who will introduce and begin the initiation of the planned changes? What employee groups will be affected? What are the timelines in which to complete the changes? How will this information be communicated to those affected? What is the anticipated reaction to the changes, once they are announced? Will employee morale and productivity be affected? These are some of the many questions that should be addressed and discussed when planning important changes.

One of the most important strategic questions that should be thoroughly discussed is how will the information be communicated to employees? What communication channels will be used? The following communication methods can be considered when planning changes: 1) Departmental meetings; 2) An employee newsletter; 3) Letters to the homes of all of the employees affected, signed by the president or general manager, whichever is appropriate; 4) An "open-door policy" for anyone wishing to have his or her questions answered.

When feasible, leaders should schedule and conduct a "state of the business" meeting with employees.

Chapter 17

How to Conduct an Effective, Useful, and Purpose-driven Meeting

When conducting a scheduled meeting, the following administrative steps should be adhered to by the person conducting the meeting and the attending participants.

Every meeting should have a Leader. He or she may go under the name of chairperson, ranking executive, manager, chief executive officer, or supervisor. The outcome of any meeting hinges on this individual's leadership ability.

These are the steps to conduct a meeting:

- Announce the meeting seven to ten days in advance.
- The advanced announcement should be communicated in such a way that would be normal to the culture (e.g., email, memo).
- Start and end the meeting on time, without exception.
- Consider starting with a short ice-breaker in order to get the attendees to feel comfortable with each other and to prepare for the agenda.
- The person chairing the meeting should try to involve every individual in attendance. The Chair may require training to better understand group dynamics.

- If action items are assigned to various participants, it is important to establish a completion date for each action.
- If the existing culture is accustomed to having Minutes recorded for future reference and filing, minutes should be taken during the meeting.

The following is a list of symptoms of communication problems that may occur when meetings are not run properly:

- Confusion in the implementation of decisions.
- An increase in subordinate demands for personal contact.
- A need to repeat communication later.
- Unaccountable increases in mistakes.
- An increase in the general anxiety level associated with employee uncertainty with regard to their future.
- Rumors and increased activity of the employee "grapevine."
- An employee who makes frequent demands on his or her manager for reassurance of understanding.

Managers should consider doing the following to improve communication within the organization:

- Hold regular group meetings.
- Communicate in language employees can understand.
- Don't always depend on the written word alone.
- Have frequent, direct face-to-face contact with employees.
- Consider your employees your most valuable resource.
- Consider holding departmental meetings with all employees.
- Senior Management should hold "state of the business" meetings with all employees, annually or every six months.

It is important to note that "uncertainty" is the opposite of information. Full Communication is achieved when the receiver understands the full meaning of the message as it was intended by the sender. This must include not only the content, as carried by the words, but also special meanings that may have a purpose related to the words used.

> Communication is one of the most important elements of good leadership, yet it is one of the least used and understood. Don't manage by "muzzling employees."

The absence of quality communication will make leadership incomplete.

Chapter 18

Team or Group Brainstorming

The team or group brainstorming process is often used not only as a meeting "ice breaker" but also as a powerful technique designed to generate a large number of ideas through interaction among group members or team members. As an important part of this administrative process, the facilitator has the responsibility of encouraging teamwork and creativity. The ideal outcomes that may result from this process are the following:

- During the brainstorm meeting:
    - The topic or problem is clarified by the participating members.
    - Ideas are never criticized.
    - All ideas are recorded.
- The idea list is narrowed down.
- A detailed discussion is held to discuss the practicality and cost of the various ideas.
- One idea is selected and discussed for evaluation and implementation.

Lastly, it is important to emphasize that for this process to be useful and effective, the facilitator and participating members must be trained in basic components of the brain-storming process. Unless there is commitment to accomplish this kind of training, the brainstorm meetings may be ineffective, or even a waste of time.

For an example of a Brainstorming Activity Sheet, please refer to page 136.

Chapter 19

Leadership Fundamentals

A leader must inspire trust.

A leader should be a good teacher and communicator.

A leader should be a problem solver.

A leader must know how to manage time well and use
it effectively.

A leader must have technical competence to effectively lead
teams and accomplish the necessary goals.

A leader must know the importance of providing vision and
mission for the organization.

A leader must know how to conduct effective and productive
meetings in order to complete the agenda in a timely fashion.

A leader must be approachable for all subordinates
and managers.

A leader should have a sense of humor.

A leader should be reliable.

A leader should display a high level of integrity at all times.

A leader must understand the importance of motivating employees, and knowledge about how to do it.

A leader should be open minded, and try to see the merit the ideas of others, even when they conflict with his or her own.

A leader freely gives positive and helpful feedback to employees.

A leader encourages excellent performance, and gives credit where it is due. When mistakes are made, a leader knows how to become an effective coach, and helps employees to learn from their mistakes.

A leader regularly establishes departmental and individual objectives to ensure that the mission of the department is successfully met.

A leader's communication is personalized so that each employee knows there is an interest in him or her.

A leader is always seeking new procedures in an effort to improve the overall performance of the organization.

A leader knows the importance of asking employees for advice or suggestions about how to improve processes or procedures, and how to address problems.

Nothing can take the place of persistence in achieving positive outcomes.

Chapter 20

Why Do People Work?

Why do people work in the world? People need to work in the world to feel like they have purpose in their lives. Ever since the beginning of time, mankind had a purpose—to survive. In the very beginning, it was food, water, and shelter. As primitive as it may have been, we did survive. As time went on, we discovered fire and began to depend heavily upon it for survival.

As the centuries passed, people became more advanced within different cultures. New discoveries were made. Advanced technologies were developed through scientific research. However, the need to survive continued, even though we were also working to find happiness.

So, once again, why do people work? Why do most people need a purpose in their lives?

Without a sense of belonging, or a feeling that they are needed, people feel superfluous. This affects their attitude and self-esteem. Within the definition of leadership, attitude is everything. Attitude is the very foundation of a leader's thought process. Leaders should have a positive attitude with which to inspire, communicate, and lead people. The responsibility of leading is to reach predetermined goals—to accomplish something, to be productive in some way, whether large or small.

This sounds like common sense to anyone who is responsible for leading people. Why, then, is leadership and maintaining a positive attitude so difficult? Could it be a lack of training? Is it possible the wrong people are in the wrong positions? Is it possible that the work environment is so negative that leaders can't make a difference no matter what they try to do? Perhaps each of these reasons plays a part.

The twenty-first century is about change and intervention. To be successful, leaders must have the necessary skill and confidence to lead.

Chapter 21

Depository of Truth

The most critical seeds leadership must cultivate are trust and integrity. If leaders are to build and maintain credibility within their departments, organizations, and corporations, they must be trusted. Trust and integrity are the key underpinnings people rely upon. Without these two components, motivation and productivity may be negatively affected, communications may be less effective and, in time, employee turnover could increase. Employees may request transfers to other departments within the organization, or leave for positions with other organizations.

Leaders are partially defined by their ability to establish and build trust and integrity. How can this be accomplished?

First, believability, trust, and integrity are important characteristics that leaders need. The leader may require training to cultivate these characteristics.

Second, the leader must demonstrate these important values when leading their teams.

Once implemented, results in teamwork, productivity, morale, quality, and turnover measures will all improve.

Chapter 22

Definition of Organizational Health

The following overview is used to describe the culture of an organization and its "Organizational Health." Most organizations take advantage of only a very small percentage of the knowledge, experience, training, and education that is available to them in their existing workforce. This is truly unfortunate! If the right environment is created by senior management—senior management must always set the example—employees will be encouraged to share their ideas to the benefit of the organization. Very few organizations invest enough of their time, energy, and planning to create such an environment.

The ability to build this kind of environment is, in my view, a characteristic of proactive, great leaders. To unlock employees' hidden talents and potential, senior management must decide that this approach would be a useful part of their strategic plans.

If employees harbor a mistrust of management, one way to improve the situation is to involve them in decision-making. By allowing employees to become involved, leaders will be able to improve their understanding of employees' needs and problems. This will also encourage employees to seek new ideas to existing problems, which will help leaders improve many of their systems and policies. Employee involvement is a management philosophy and process that encourages, allows, or requires employees to become involved in some aspects of management decision-making. This approach, if administered effectively, helps management develop more innovative solutions to existing problems, which could also mean cost savings, improvements in product or service quality, improved morale, and so on.

There is no one particular employee involvement program that will satisfy all of the organization's needs because each organization is unique.

When senior managers decide to begin an employee involvement program, they need to decide on a type of program that will help them to achieve their near-term and long-term strategic plans, and which employees will be selected to participate. Leadership concepts are easy to create and to implement; however, they are very difficult and complicated to administer.

A proactive leader must have a thorough understanding of these concepts, the employees that he or she manages, the effects their implementation may have on the team, and how to measure the results, once implemented.

At the center of every culture are visions of the future and values that guide behavior within an organization. Also, within every culture are fundamental elements such as organizational structure, systems, skills, management styles, and values that support the organization's vision and mission. These fundamental elements are the building blocks that will help shape or re-shape the organization's culture and establish cohesion among departments and the various teams within each of the departments.

If this kind of major change in the culture is to be successful, the management and the employees need to be totally committed from the very beginning. This may require a major change in the way the company traditionally conducts business. Without clear management commitment, employees may view management as insincere, and might not support these new processes.

At the very beginning of such a change, there must be clear communication to all employees, followed by orientation and training for those who will be involved in the program. Senior management must provide the necessary resources, time, and budgets. This may include allowing employees time away from their work areas to participate in training sessions and other necessary program components. A cost-effective reward system should also be considered.

> Leadership is like a house, something always
> needs to be fixed.

Chapter 23

Sharing Leadership

LEADERSHIP WITHOUT FENCES

Effective Leadership involves sharing important responsi-bilities with other employees who have expressed a desire to broaden their scope of responsibility and who may have the basic skills needed to lead. It is to the benefit of leaders and team members to share portions of the leadership role. This will also build self-confidence in team members, and expand their capabilities, and give the leader more confidence in the abilities of the team when the leader must be absent so that the day-to-day objectives are successfully met or even, in some cases, exceeded.

While there are various ways to exercise leadership, one of the goals of any leader should be to share the skills he or she possesses with various team members. This helps to strengthen the team. This means that an effective leader must be willing to also be a teacher. To teach implies that one is willing to try to pass one's own knowledge on to others. When this is done successfully, the self-esteem of those being taught will increase significantly. This in itself will have very positive benefits for high morale, high productivity, a more cohesive team, and an improved ability to meet goals.

Leadership is a very complex subject. The speed at which knowledge is accessible in the twenty-first century continues to astound. But this knowledge is one of the key elements to success for both leaders and employees and enables them to make valuable contributions to the organization. A learning organization is a on journey with no end.

Leaders should assess their vision and mission statements frequently, and modify them when appropriate and necessary to remain competitive. Sharing the vision and mission will create a sense of pride and purpose in all employees. Successful leaders need to realize that the financial success of their organization involves a careful balance of the technological advances of domestic and global business and the complex understanding of what motivates employees. Leaders also need to understand the importance of giving life to their vision and mission statements to ensure they will have meaning that supports the goals of the organization through their teams.

Chapter 24
Employee Counseling

Counseling that may be needed to address a team-based problem is often mistaken for criticism unless it is fully understood. Effective leaders will dispel this fear by demonstrating to team members that the intent is to help them improve in areas that require behavioral change. Counseling is a process to help managers solve operational problems, when they emerge. If done professionally and effectively by a trained manager, this will help establish an environment that will be non-threatening to employees. It reassures them that the process is needed to improve performance. It will also help each member of the team to reach his or her full potential.

Before beginning counseling, it is important that the department leader try to completely understand the situation. Leaders must listen carefully, and summarize, and then verify the facts completely to determine the root cause of the problem. Once this is completed, the leader/counselor meets with the individual or group to discuss the findings and determine the best solution to correct the problem.

The counselor's role is to give encouragement and advice to make the team more cohesive and help them work together to address the performance issues. A "cup" of this kind of leadership helps improve employee behavior, change negative attitudes, improve morale, increase productivity, and reduce employee turnover.

If a person in a leadership position is a realist, this individual will come to understand he or she will not win them all. Managers at all levels do the best they can with the facts they have, within the policies of the organization. They make every effort to be consistent, treat employees with dignity and fairness and, at the same time, run the business they are responsible for. Counseling team members when necessary will help the team or department to become more cohesive.

Chapter 25

The Clarity of Leadership

COMMON ELEMENTS

There are a number of common leadership elements that each manager needs to develop as an effective manager. Additional information can be found in chapter 19, page 68. The importance of leadership has been recognized since the very early times. Effective leadership is the key that can mean the difference between the success and failure of any business. Proactive leadership is the influencing of others within a department to work willingly toward achieving pre-determined objectives. Defining the elements of leadership within the desired leadership style is critically important to ensure that the leader is the appropriate choice for operational and strategic reasons.

Selecting the right leader will affect the organizational health of a department, company, or a senior management at the corporate level. These staffing choices can help transform unhealthy organizations to healthy ones.

The key result of this transformation will be cohesive teams. This is also a way to intellectualize the various components of the culture without bureaucratizing it through the various elements of proactive leadership.

Albert Einstein once said, "No new problem can be solved by the same consciousness that created it. We need to see the world anew."

The following is a list of attributes and activities of successful leadership:

- Vision and Mission
- Trust / Honesty / Integrity / Honor
- Building Teams / Teamwork
- Goals and objectives
- Global focus
- Morals / Ethics
- Communication, written, verbal, non-verbal
- Leadership thinking skills / Being proactive
- Customer service orientation
- Conducting effective meetings
- Coaching / Counseling
- Training / Creating a learning organization
- Employee involvement
- Implementing change
- Effective recruiting
- Open-door policy
- Respect for others
- Creating synergy with other departments, suppliers, and customers
- Physical vitality and stamina
- Ability to motivate
- Conflict resolution skills
- Problem-solving process Skills
- Strategic thinking / planning near-term and long-term
- Financial success
- Intellectual energy and curiosity
- Situational leadership skills
- Building organizational harmony

- Social skills / Sense of humor
- Emotional intelligence

These actions and attributes give leadership
life and meaning.

Chapter 26

Leadership Thinking Skills

ARTICULATING A CLEAR SENSE OF PURPOSE

Being a leader requires more than possessing knowledge about leadership. The leader also needs to have leadership thinking skills. To thoroughly assess the performance of a team, leaders must familiarize themselves with the day-to-day operations of the business to determine which of the objectives and or strategies have been met and which of the objectives have not been met, and why. This attention to detail is a *must* if the organizational objectives are going to be successfully met. Asking why the team has not met its goals or objectives should lead to identifying what has led to the failure.

The leader must ask:

Was it human error or an equipment problem that caused the team to miss one or more completion dates?

Can the cause and effect be determined through an examination of chronological events?

What is the root cause of the problem?

After the fact-finding stage, the leader and the team must decide what should be done to address the problem and decide on a realistic and timely plan of action. This could involve restructuring the team by replacing some of the members who are not committed to the objectives of the group or adding new team members. This approach may also involve consulting with different departments to determine more of the facts that may have had a negative impact on the teams' efforts. The leader must find the right solution (situational leadership) to correct the problem so that the team can meet its objectives.

Leaders should always strive to create camaraderie among employees.

Chapter 27

Role Modeling

R ole Modeling is a very important part of leadership in all business segments. Setting an example is one of the most important leadership skills a leader needs. As the expression goes "we hear what leaders say, but we watch what they do." Modeling is one of the most effective ways to show others the proper way in which to conduct themselves. In business, it is usually not just what leaders say, but what they do that will most influence and shape employees' behavior.

Leaders will display their value system and it will be obvious to the employees in the group, department, or team. Role modeling will influence the team members' trust of their leader and their ability to perform cohesively to meet the predetermined objectives successfully. This will also help by building self-confidence in team members. The leader's role includes sharing of authority, and ensuring that the team has the tools and information needed to perform effectively and successfully.

This is the real world of business. Leadership in the modern world is not a simple activity—it is much more complex than just telling people what to do. The leader develops and communicates a shared vision of the future with the team members. This cannot be accomplished without trust. There is a correlation between trust and role modeling. Successful role modeling cannot exist without trust. This is an important underpinning for the work environment to be positive and for the employees to be motivated.

It is extremely important that leaders lead by example if they are to influence others.

Chapter 28

Leadership and Planning

Planning is necessary at all levels in an organization. Planning is an essential element of leadership in all segments of business and involves leaders and team members. The planning process is essential if the various teams are to achieve the goals and objectives that have been established within each of their departments.

Many organizations have found it necessary and useful to establish, in writing, one-year plans, three-year plans, and five-year plans. These plans include resources, timelines, goals, and written objectives, and, if achieved, what the desired result will be. When complete, these plans provide direction, timelines, and completion dates, and goals can be met successfully when performed by cohesive teams. The leader will be accountable for the implementation and administration of the plans. It is very common for organizations to have weekly or monthly staff meetings to discuss progress toward these goals.

Depending on the organizational structure, the senior management members report to a general manager, chief executive officer, or president. The reporting structure of senior management could include departments such as marketing, human resources, finance, engineering, manu-facturing, research and development, and international sales and marketing. This list of departments is representative of a high-technology, manufacturing organization. Other types of business may use a different list of departments.

For example, in the hospitality business—specifically hotels—the senior management staff, also known as the executive committee, would be comprised of representatives of marketing, finance, rooms, food and beverage, human resources, and engineering. The leaders in those positions report to a general manager of the hotel.

In the health care industry, the senior management staff includes representatives of nursing, finance, human resources, radiology, engineering, marketing, patient rela-tions, plus a senior medical staff member.

These are the senior management team members that provide leadership, guidance, and direction for each of these industries. They steer the ship, so to speak, using a predeter-mined strategic compass that encompasses the vision and mission statements.

For senior management staff meetings, the agenda requires that the members be prepared to discuss the progress of their goals and objectives, and the overall status of each of their departments. This may be done using PowerPoint, flip charts, or conversation around a board table. Whatever the method used, this process will provide updates on the goals and objectives, and also gives other members of the senior management team the opportunity to be updated, and to ask questions of each presenter.

If the process is communicated and effectively admin-istered, each member of the senior management team will contribute with updates about the department he or she is responsible for, and how their work continues to support the goals and objectives of the organization. Typically, at the beginning of a new business year—fiscal or calendar—each of the senior management team submits a plan or a white paper that specifically describes what he or she plans to accomplish during the next twelve months. This report is then submitted to the person to whom she or he reports—president, general manager, chief executive officer, hospital administrator, and so on.

After these plans are approved in writing, they are then communicated to all of the members of each discipline. This process and the maintenance of good relationships among the senior management team members is critical to the organization's success. Members must be committed to working well together, and to taking ownership for their goals and objectives, based on the position they hold in the organization. Owners hold a high degree of responsibility for their parts of the operation. Leadership through partnership with each of the senior management team members, direct reports, and the employees in each of these departments will enable the organization to be successful.

A visionary leader will need to adapt plans to handle unexpected changes to avoid non-optimal outcomes.

Chapter 29

Creating Balance in Your Life Between Work and Exercise

Many managers and employees spend a great deal of time at work, and it is extremely important to have a schedule that includes some form of exercise.

The normal schedule for a full-time employee is 2,000 hours a year. That is a significant amount of time to spend at your place of employment. Although it is important to remain committed and focused on one's job, earning a living and displaying your commitment, it is also important to form good exercise habits. To provide effective leadership, managers need a way to maintain physical fitness and increase physical strength.

Between work, family, maintaining a home, and perhaps traveling, Time Management may help a great deal to plan the time needed for some form of physical activity. The physical activities could include walking, riding a bike, swimming, rowing a boat, and so on.

During the last decade, research has shown that exercise has the potential of reducing stress and tension, and it doesn't require more than twenty to thirty minutes a day. However, to be of any benefit, it must be scheduled on a regular basis.

According to exercise physiologists, exercise also tends to build a healthier self-concept. People who exercise often feel better about themselves and may become more self-confident.

One of the keys to a regular exercise program is to choose something that you enjoy. In the beginning, goals should be small and achievable. Consider keeping an exercise log or journal. This provides detailed information about your exercise program and could help you stay motivated. Remember: When changing your diet or beginning a new fitness program, it is advisable to seek medical advice from your physician, especially if you are currently taking any prescription medicines.

Leaders need to make time in their day for a
period of solitude.

Chapter 30

Emotional Intelligence and Leadership

Business leaders at all levels are faced with a large amount of information for use in making effective, professional decisions. The decisions they make could have far reaching consequences, from the perception of their leadership, to the effectiveness of their teams, and even the success of the organization. In this regard, leaders are dealing with complex information while trying to run the business efficiently every day. This information typically includes the employees they supervise, their customers, quality issues, production issues, and the costs of doing business. Sometimes more research is required on a given topic for the information to be complete.

Acquiring knowledge is extremely important, but how we use it is even more important. Understanding Emotional Intelligence can be an advantage for managers when leading people, building teams, and working toward meeting organizational and departmental objectives. It is a critical skill for success as a leader.

For leaders to inspire and motivate their teams, they must have the desire, knowledge, and ability to provide leadership within their scope of responsibility. I strongly believe that these attributes should start at the very top of the organization and be visible throughout the culture. This can be viewed as role modeling throughout the organization, which is also an important component of proactive leadership.

It is also important for leaders to understand the various behavior patterns of the employees they supervise, including their emotions, problems they may be experiencing on the job, and various needs the employees have. Leaders must get to know employees on an individual basis, not personally, but professionally. They must also follow the rules and regulations set out in the formal Employee Handbook. This requires emotional intelligence as well.

Relevant knowledge should precede important decisions and actions, and life-long learning helps avoid "mental sclerosis" or "hardening of the attitudes," terms used by Linda and Charlie Bloom in their blog, "Building Relationship Skills." Emotional intelligence is key to successful teamwork.

Managing with good decisions and emotional intelligence is not easy. It takes a great deal of hard work and requires credibility and persistence. The end result will be the acceptance of this kind of leadership, higher morale, improved quality and productivity, lower turnover, and much better efficiency throughout the organization. Don't wait for conditions to be perfect to work on good decision-making and improving your understanding of your team members' needs—conditions will never be perfect.

Managers can expect obstacles and difficulties, and these should be solved as they arise. Ideas alone won't bring change and success to the organization. Ideas have value only when they are implemented, followed up, and when corrective action is taken as needed.

Develop good habits and make them
your masters.

93

Chapter 31

Leadership Reborn

RESTORING THE BALANCE OF LEADERSHIP

Acquiring knowledge is extremely important. How we use it is even more important. Understanding Emotional Intelligence can clearly be an advantage for managers when leading people, building teams, and working towards meeting organizational and departmental objectives. Having this knowledge is a critical skill necessary to be successful as a leader. The mind once expanded to dimensions of larger ideas and knowledge, never returns to its original size. In a way this is an approach to avoid mental sclerosis or hardening of the attitudes, a term referred to by Linda and Charlie Bloom in their blog, "Building Relationship Skills." This approach is also an important key to teamwork. Relevant knowledge should always precede important decisions and actions. Perhaps another way to state it would be "Leadership through Partnership." These ideas, in part, are ways in which to avoid stagnation. One can't steer an ocean liner with a canoe paddle.

Develop good habits and make them
your masters.

Chapter 32

The Uncertainty of Business

PRESCRIPTION FOR LEADERSHIP

If the unexpected should happen, which it frequently does in business, will your organization be ready? Will your senior managers know how to make important business decisions? Will the various departments and teams be prepared to resolve the issues they face?

These are just a few of the questions that business leaders should ask themselves. If teams aren't trained to effectively address the uncertainty and the variety of issues that need to be resolved, what is needed to make them ready? This requires a strategic vision and mission. If an organization meets the needs of employees, they will meet the needs of the business. Of course, this must be known and understood by all the managers within the organization.

Conclusion

As we come to the end of the Pocket Guide, it is our hope that you find the contents meaningful and useful. You must go forward as a learner if you want to go forward as a leader. Wisdom is the continuous acquisition of knowledge, facts, and the desire to keep learning.

Remember, if the organization meets the needs
of the employees, the employees will meet the
needs of the organization. In the end it's all
about people.

Leadership Case Studies

In creating these hypothetical leadership case studies, the author used examples acquired in his many years of teaching in college and university. These case studies are intended to supplement the conceptual material and to help readers to understand the leadership processes more completely, and to help develop critical thinking skills.

All case studies are completely fictitious.

Case Study A

HEALTH CARE ORGANIZATION – AUTOCRATIC LEADERSHIP STYLE

The vice president of Nursing in a small hospital in the Northeastern part of the United States was very autocratic, dictatorial, and controlling. She had earned quite a negative reputation, and was feared by the nursing staff at all levels. The president of the hospital had warned her on a number of occasions to change her approach when interacting with those in her department. The hospital was non-union and had tried to promote an open-door policy to ensure that managers heard the concerns of all employees, including the nursing organization.

The Human Resources vice president (HRVP) had taken a proactive approach for many years to ensure that the hospital remained non-union, in addition to making every effort to increase morale throughout the hospital. There were numerous occasions that required the HRVP to talk to the VP of Nursing about concerns being expressed by various members of the nursing staff. After a period of time, the relationship between the HRVP and the VP of Nursing had become one of conflict and awkwardness. The VP of Nursing was essentially in denial, and she wasn't willing to make a genuine effort to change her leadership style. This, of course, was very problematic. The HRVP had created a file and was documenting every meeting with the VP of Nursing.

The complaints and concerns continued for a long time, and the morale of the nursing staff was at an all-time low. To keep the president of the hospital up to date, he was briefed periodically on the details of each meeting. The president was very concerned, but he wasn't willing to take disciplinary action of any kind.

Morale was very low and rumors were circulating about needing a union to represent the nursing staff. This became a very serious concern of the president, members of the Board of Directors, and other members of management. Once a union campaign begins, efforts to prevent a business from becoming unionized is mentally and physically difficult.

The key person for this effort is usually the HRVP, and he took the lead. He had begun to schedule meetings with the nurse managers without the VP of Nursing being present. This decision was supported by the president of the hospital and the chairman of the board, and recommended by the HRVP. As the meetings were scheduled and held and chaired by the HRVP, and information was being gathered and summarized for analysis, and for the purpose of making logical decisions.

The findings clearly pointed to a lack of proactive leadership by the VP of Nursing. Her behavior was very negative and demeaning, and showed a lack of caring for her staff, and a lack of quality communication. Performance reviews were always late and negative, and staff meetings were seldom held. The data was summarized by the HRVP and reported to the president of the hospital and the chairman of the Board. The concerns were discussed and it was agreed that an important decision had to be made.

The options that were discussed were the following:

1. Should we put her on probation for the next ninety days to give her a chance to change her leadership style?

2. Should we offer her an early retirement package to encourage her to leave her position?
3. Should we consider termination?

It is important to point out that there was enough documentation to legally warrant termination. The documentation had been gathered during a period of months in the meetings chaired by the HRVP. Obviously, quality of nursing in any hospital is critical and is associated with the hospital's mission statement. When the nursing staff morale is low, the quality of patient care can be jeopardized because the self-esteem of the nurses has been negatively affected. A person's self-esteem and motivation are closely tied together.

These options were discussed with the VP of Nursing in a meeting with the HRVP and the president of the hospital, and she decided to take the early retirement option.

A timeline was established for her departure and the recruiting effort began to replace her with a qualified health care professional as quickly as possible. When the nursing staff learned of her decision to retire, the morale quickly improved. Additionally, the rumors of a union campaign disappeared.

Lessons

This kind of behavioral leadership problem should not have been allowed to exist for as long as it did—several years, in this case. The problem should have been addressed by the VP of Nursing's supervisor and the president as soon as it became known that her leadership style was negative and autocratic. Her approach clearly had a direct negative effect upon the nurses in the department—their motivation, self-esteem, and overall daily performance all suffered.

This case study demonstrates the importance of modern leadership in health care and all organizations. There is no short cut to providing sound leadership and direction to teams. Leadership requires dedication, credibility, and hard work by all managers who have the responsibility of leading teams of people.

Case Study B

HEALTH CARE ADMINISTRATOR/CEO – PROBLEM AVOIDANCE

An Administrator/CEO in a large hospital clearly did not understand the importance of providing complete, proactive leadership for the hospital that he was responsible for, especially in the areas where there were obvious employee problems. He consistently displayed signs of burnout and avoidance behavior in the daily operation of the hospital. Employee problems were ignored and left to his direct reports to resolve in all departments in the hospital.

This health care institution was a non-union facility; the Human Resources vice president and his staff tried to maintain an open-door policy for the employees to allow them to discuss their concerns or frustrations with management. This task, at times, became overwhelming because the administrator was not willing to address problems. Frustration and uncertainty had been building for several years.

Members of the Board of Directors became aware of these significant problems, and had begun to question why these issues weren't being addressed and resolved. The pressure had begun to build on the administrator, and his behavior and leadership was being questioned. Numerous meetings were held with his direct reports to keep him up to date about employee concerns.

He had begun to lose credibility among his direct reports and the employees of the hospital. His lack of leadership had become very obvious; employee morale was at an all-time low as a result of problems not being dealt with. He was spending much more time in his office, and he was not focusing on the serious problems that were being brought to his attention on an almost daily basis.

Teamwork and quality communication among departments were eroding and there was concern that the quality of care for patients would start to suffer. The administrator was more concerned with politics and pleasing the Board of Directors than he was with performing the important duties of his job as the administrator of the hospital.

Morale continued to deteriorate, turnover became a costly concern, and employees were extremely frustrated that the very visible problems weren't being addressed and resolved.

The hospital Board of Directors and the hospital administrator had begun to schedule meetings to discuss various approaches to address and resolve these problems. After a number of monthly meetings with the Board of Directors, various options were discussed. The Board of Directors and the hospital president agreed to hire a management consultant to help correct the problems the employees had been raising.

When the management consulting team was hired, they began with fact-finding; For three months, the consultants gathered information about the problems the employees had been reporting for the previous eighteen months.

After the data was formulated, assessed, and discussed, it was agreed that the next step would be to schedule an Employee Attitude Survey, also called an Employer Vulnerability Audit. This survey is an instrument that is used to ask employees to express their concerns with regard to their work culture.

The Board of Directors and the president of the hospital agreed that schedules would be established and communicated to all employees for completion of the survey to gather their opinions.

Employees were told when they could complete the survey, and the news was met with a great deal of enthusiasm—employees were very receptive. The general opinion within the hospital among the employees was that finally their concerns would be heard and action would be taken to improve their work environment.

The survey form was designed to be confidential, so employee names were not required on the form. The surveys were filled in by all staff over a period of a week to ensure that all shifts had the opportunity to express their opinions.

In the general case, the purpose of conducting a confidential Employee Attitude Survey is threefold: 1) to find out the present level of employee morale for the organization, and for each survey group, 2) to find out how effectively the organization is meeting the needs of employee job satisfaction, 3) to solicit employees' suggestions about what can be done to make the organization an even better place to work for everyone. The ultimate objective in conducting an Employee Attitude Survey is improvement in employee attitude and morale, improving the employer-employee relationships, and increasing overall efficiency in the quality of services provided.

The following topics were addressed in the hospital employee survey:

- Top management attitudes toward morale
- Supervisory attitudes toward employees
- Human Resource policies
- Working conditions
- Employee benefits
- Compensation polices
- Job security
- Safety

- Complaint and grievance procedure
- Consistency of organizational rules and discipline
- Leadership and supervision
- Employee Handbook and Policy Manual
- Bulletin boards

After the data was compiled and assessed, it was very clear that hospital leadership needed to change their approach and the overall work environment if employee morale was to improve.

Action plans were put in place by all departments to make the changes necessary to accomplish these goals. The Board of Directors were made aware of the findings from the survey and had agreed to implement the various departmental action plans.

Lessons

The key point of this case is the need for training and leadership to meet the needs of all employees. There is no shortcut to accomplishing this goal. The leadership must start at the top with the senior management, and communicate the objectives throughout the organization. This effort required credibility, hard work, accountability, and purposeful communication, including an open-door policy for all employees.

Case Study C

HOSPITALITY INDUSTRY – GENERAL MANAGER INACTION

This case involves a large corporate hotel organization. Senior management in the hospitality industry is called the Executive Committee. The Executive Committee positions are: General Manager, Food and Beverage Director, Director of Engineering, Director of Housekeeping, Director of Human Resources, Director of Marketing and Sales, and Director of Finance. The size of the hotel property is determined by the number of rooms that are available in the hotel. This was a large hotel with close to a thousand rooms.

In this hotel, the Human Resources department was structured in such a way that each of the functions had a manager reporting to the Human Resources Vice President (HRVP). When the new HRVP was hired, he had to learn the various components of the culture, and rebuild the Human Resources team. He also had to get to know the various managers and how they ran their individual departments, including their management styles, and how they contributed to the hotel's services. Note that the hotel employees were not unionized, and it is especially important to meet the needs of each employee if possible and affordable.

After getting an understanding of how the hotel worked, the new HRVP began to hold the managers accountable for achieving each of their goals on an annual basis.

The HRVP began to hold staff meetings once a week. The discussions revolved around the various action items assigned to each manager. This was a good way to communicate with each manager, to make the team stronger, and to ensure provision of high-quality hotel services.

At about eight months into the new HRVP's tenure, this approach began to be met with some resistance by several of the managers, and became a political issue. This became evident when several of the managers arranged a private meeting with the general manager of the hotel. This meeting did not involve the HRVP.

This is not the professional way to resolve the situation. It is important to note that the approach the new HRVP was using to run the Human Resource Department was the process mandated by the general manager when the HRVP was hired.

The HRVP became frustrated and disappointed upon learning of the meetings that did not include him. After a period of just over two years, he resigned for another position.

Lessons

The general manager should have involved the HRVP in the meetings to ensure that the concerns being expressed were accurate, and not political or emotional. In business, there are always multiple sides to a story. Leadership in any business should involve effective communication to ensure that everyone is treated fairly and professionally and with dignity. This did not happen in this case.

What should have happened is the following: The hotel general manager should have tried to retrieve all the facts related to the allegations being made against the HRVP. He didn't do this. Also, a meeting should have been facilitated by the general manager, the HRVP, and the managers to learn the facts.

The key lessons here include the importance of providing leadership, objectivity, effective communications, and taking the time to learn the facts involving the allegations. The general manager's approach was wrong and ineffective. The outcome was a poor one in the sense that the truth was never determined and the managers were never held accountable.

Case Study D

HEALTH CARE – LACK OF EMPLOYEE PERFORMANCE REVIEWS

The hospital discussed in this case study employed three hundred full-time people and one hundred part-time people. Senior management included the following professionals: President, Vice President of Nursing, Vice President of Finance, Human Resources Vice President, Director of Engineering and Maintenance, Director of Dietary, Director of Housekeeping, and the Director of the Medical Staff.

Over a period spanning several years, employee performance reviews were not being conducted in a timely way. This was allowed to happen because the president did not provide the necessary leadership to ensure the performance review process was being administered correctly and on time for all employees. He allowed the system to fail by not requiring his direct reports to give employee reviews the priority they warrant.

Over time, employee morale was negatively affected. When morale is poor, motivation is decreased. The employees began to think that senior management didn't care about their individual performance. This topic came up in regular discussions among employees, and it had a far-reaching affect in the following areas:

- Morale deteriorated.
- Motivation decreased.
- Turnover increased.

Private discussions begin on the subject of establishing a union; union cards began to be seen in the hospital.

Lessons

This kind of problem can be avoided if senior management makes timely performance reviews a priority. Some of the reasons why performance reviews are not done:

> Managers may not be trained to conduct performance review interviews.

> Senior management has not communicated and emphasized the importance of performance reviews, and that they be completed on a timely basis.

> The administrative system may be flawed in the sense that the Human Resources Department doesn't send out the reviews to departmental managers on a schedule, and this causes a backlog.

> Department managers may not exercise good time management skills, which prevents them from making the time to do the reviews.

Patient Care is the Highest Priority

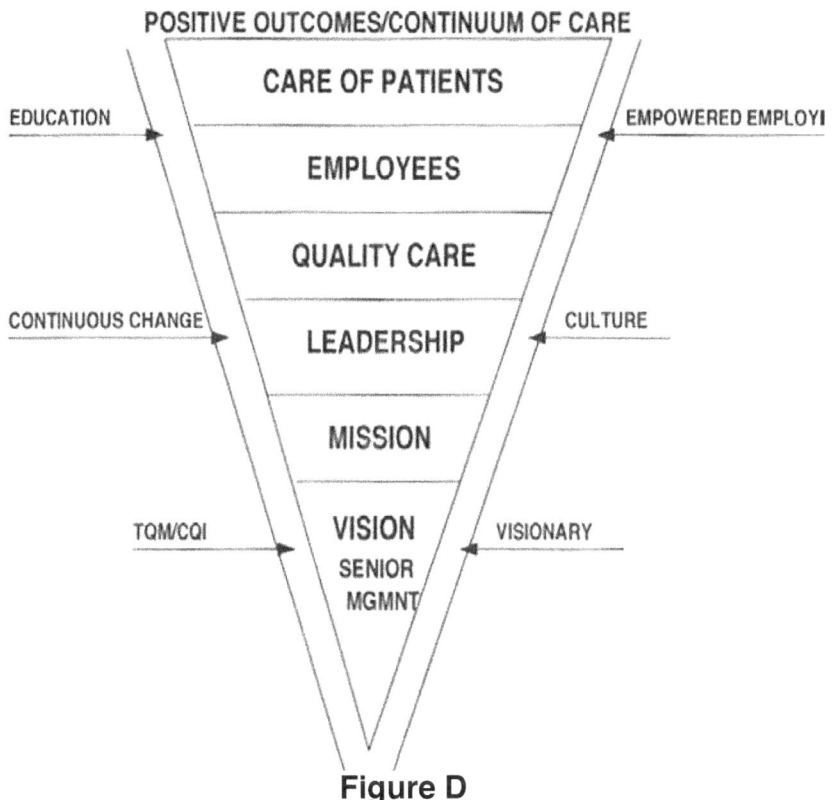

Figure D

Case Study E

HIGH TECHNOLOGY
(BUSINESS EQUIPMENT)
– INADEQUATE COMMUNICATION

This case is unique and interesting because it involves a high technology manufacturing, sales, and marketing organization. The manufacturing plant is non-union, and management has worked very hard to ensure that the plant remains non-union. During recent years, there have been attempts to unionize this particular plant, but they were unsuccessful.

The senior management staff consists of the following: President, Vice President of Finance, Vice President of Marketing, Human Resources Vice President (HRVP), Vice President of Manufacturing, Vice President of Engineering, and Vice President of Research and Development. The organization employs six hundred people at this location. The president reports directly to the president of the corporation located in another state.

Financially, this plant is doing very well, and is very stable. They have avoided lay-offs for quite some time. In fact, the organization is still hiring people for some of the hourly positions in manufacturing and some administrative positions, and a number of professional positions. This is always a good indication of how the organization is doing financially.

A major concern that senior management consistently expressed was the continuous need to improve morale, especially among the hourly employees. Brainstorming sessions were held to try to find ways to accomplish this. The Human Resources Director (HRD) who was charged with doing this was constantly finding logical and responsive ways to keep morale high.

As part of the initiative to improve morale, a quarterly Employee Communications Meeting was introduced to improve communication. These meetings continued for a three-year period and the results were excellent. The hourly employees were selected by their department manager on a rotating basis, and they attended, prepared to ask questions about any topic they felt was important. The questions were gathered from each employee in each of the departments, who gave them to the person selected to attend the meetings. Each meeting lasted no longer than one hour.

The meetings started with the HRD welcoming all of the employees to the meeting. In attendance was a Human Resources secretary, who recorded all of the questions that were asked. The HRD answered questions as completely as possible. Once the meeting was over, the questions were reviewed during the following week, and each of the questions was answered thoroughly. Questions and answers would be typed utilizing a report format, and posted on all bulletin boards to communicate the questions and answers to all employees.

Due to the emergence of difficult economic business conditions for the company, a new performance review and compensation policy was mandated for all six hundred employees. The HRD was given the difficult responsibility of communicating and administering this policy. It was a nightmare, to say the least! The HRVP, also located at this facility, did not assist in any way. This situation became political and very problematic.

All of the other senior management for each department, and their direct reports did not accept the new policy easily. This being the case, the major responsibility for administering it was placed upon the HRD without any support. The hourly employees were very upset, and would not accept the changes. This affected morale, motivation, attitudes, and the quality of the work. Hourly employees, especially, became extremely negative.

The HRD strongly suggested that each of the senior managers hold group meetings to inform employees so they would better understand why the new policy had to be implemented. The managers were not receptive to this idea, stating they were much too busy to be bothered with these kinds of meetings, that it was the responsibility of Human Resources. The HRVP, once again, would not get involved.

After a few weeks, there was some talk of a union campaign among the hourly employees, mostly in the factory. This led to private union meetings at alternate locations—restaurants or employees' homes. The situation escalated to the point that union authorization cards were seen in the plant, along with requests that employees sign them.

The corporate office, located several hundred miles away, became extremely concerned, and a law firm was hired to stop the union campaign. They were very professional and experienced. The attorneys scheduled numerous meetings with different groups of employees to determine the root cause of the effort to unionize.

The main reason was found to be the new compensation policy. The new policy was intended to save money, and a high percentage of employees would not get an increase for at least another year. Employees found this very difficult, if not impossible, to accept. This disappointment led to other issues such as the health care policy, the internal promotion policy, the lack of effective leadership by the first line supervisors, not enough equipment and tools to do their job, and more. These are the issues that emerged during the attorneys' investigation.

These serious problems lasted for about a year. There were numerous meetings with all employees, coordinated by the HRD and the attorneys. This process was very time-consuming and expensive. However, progress was being made in addressing the employees' concerns. The root cause of all the employees' discontent was the limited amount of money that had been budgeted for performance review and related compensation increases. The concerns were compiled and disseminated to all senior management, and to the corporate office.

After these concerns were analyzed, it was decided that the previous performance review schedule would be reinstated. Monies were allocated as necessary to stop the union campaign. Additionally, many other issues were addressed: the health care plan was improved, the necessary tools were provided for the various departments, and leadership training was instituted for the first line supervisors. When these changes were implemented, all of the selling points of the union were eliminated, and the campaign eventually stopped.

Lessons

- Senior management should have been more responsible; they should have scheduled all the meetings necessary to ensure that employees understood the reasons for the change.
- The HRVP should have helped take the lead to assist the HRD in addressing employee concerns.
- Plant-wide meetings should have been scheduled and held to address the many questions the employees had.

There is no substitute for proactive leadership for meeting the needs of employees. This can only be accomplished through commitment, effective communications, and a thorough understanding of the needs of the employees. This situation could have been avoided if leadership, professionalism, and common sense were utilized.

Case Study F

HIGH TECHNOLOGY-DEFENSE
INDUSTRY – AUTOCRATIC PRESIDENT

This case involves a high technology defense division that was highly structured. Reporting to the President of this division were: Vice President of Manufacturing, Vice President of Engineering, Vice President of Human Resources, Director of Research and Development, Director of Public Relations, Vice President of Marketing, Vice President of Finance, and Director of Maintenance.

The division was very successful technologically and financially. Their marketing programs were very effective, and they often attracted government contracts. The plant facilities were modern, and the necessary maintenance for equipment was always given priority to ensure the equipment was operating safely and properly. All of the Occupational Safety Standards were strictly enforced and administered. The plant employed 1,500 people, of which 1,000 were hourly employees and non-union.

The leadership style employed by the president was mostly Theory X or "management by fear." This individual was very driven to be successful. When senior management meetings were conducted, the president was in control and was very demanding; staff meetings lasted four to five hours, on average.

The meetings were productive in the sense that a great deal of information was shared by each of the senior managers. This was accomplished by each manager giving a semi-formal presentation and providing copies to each of the other meeting attendees for review and future reference. The senior managers were concerned and somewhat frightened by this management style. However, they needed to work, and many of them had been there many years, so they tolerated the president's behavior, and did the best they could. Although it was very difficult at times, they performed to the best of their abilities.

Over time, the hourly employees became disgruntled, frustrated, and unhappy because of how they perceived they were being treated by the group leaders and first line supervisors. This unhappiness continued to grow and became very visible, involving changing attitudes and behaviors. The plant had two shifts scheduled in order to meet production requirements for its defense contract customers.

The Human Resources Director and others within the Human Resources Department repeatedly reported that the hourly employee unhappiness was continuing to grow. These reports were given to the president, the vice-president of Human Resources, and all other senior management members. These reports were given—in detail—over a period of time, at the scheduled senior management staff meetings.

The Human Resources Department strongly recommended that leadership training be scheduled for all management staff, and that a formal Employee Attitude Survey be scheduled for all employees. The Employee Attitude Survey is a process in which employees in all departments throughout the plant are asked a number of questions about the overall environment in which they are working.

After the Attitude Survey process is complete, the information is tabulated and the reports are disseminated to senior management for review and assessment. Once this information is reviewed and discussed, plans are made to address concerns to improve morale and motivation of the work force. After the plans and actions are finalized, employee meetings are scheduled to communicate plans in response to the Employee Attitude Survey findings.

In this case, all of these steps were accomplished. The various changes were implemented, and very importantly, this removed all the issues from the ongoing union campaign. The union campaign went away and the running of normal operations for the business continued.

Lessons

The key lesson associated with this case is to not let the various problems go unaddressed this long. Purposeful and proactive leadership is critical to ensure that the needs of employees are met where possible and affordable. If this is done on a continuous basis, the problems like those described in this case will not reach this level of seriousness.

Case Study G

INTERNATIONAL HIGH TECHNOLOGY BUSINESS EQUIPMENT COMPANY – PROBLEM AVOIDANCE

This organization was experiencing sustained annual growth internationally because of their diversified, high-quality product offerings. They continued to penetrate and capture the market as a result of sound marketing strategies, properly placed employees, hard work, and their research and development of new products for existing and new customers.

Because of their rapid growth, which included various acquisitions over a period of years, some of the operations managers did not have the necessary leadership skills. This resulted in very poor management practices in several parts of the operation. This case study will highlight the various leadership skills that appeared to be lacking in several managers, why this may have occurred, and what should have been done to correct the problems.

This specific situation involves a manager of an important manufacturing assembly operation at a distant location from the corporate office. He reports directly to the president of a division that is based at the corporate office. The division president reports the president of the corporation.

The manager of this important satellite location was part of an acquisition several years earlier. Technically, he appeared to have the skills needed to oversee the various products that were being assembled for customers, but through the previous eighteen months, this manager had not been following the established policies required to meet the quality standards. When these sub-par products arrived at the corporate office manufacturing location and were inspected for quality, they were found to be inadequate for shipping to the customers.

These issues continued to be addressed with this manager; however, he continued to perform in the same manner, and was not willing to make any changes. The division president to whom he reported kept trying to address these performance problems, but without taking any disciplinary action. The division president was displaying avoidance behavior by not addressing the root causes of the performance problems. This was clearly a serious operational mistake, because this organization had a quality reputation that was known throughout the industry—and wished to maintain it.

Lessons

The manager should have been warned that if he didn't improve his performance and meet the corporate quality standards, progressive disciplinary measures would be administered, and a complete set of chronological documentation would be placed in his file. The record of events and actions is important to protect against potential litigation.

It seemed possible that this manager did not have the leadership skills necessary to be responsible for the scope of his operation. In this case, he should have either been put on probation, reassigned, or terminated for cause.

The key lesson in this case study is to not let this kind of performance issue go unaddressed once the problems are known.

Case Study H

A WELL-KNOWN UNIVERSITY – POOR QUALITY TEACHING

Several full-time faculty members and the Dean were holding strategic planning meetings to discuss plans for the forthcoming school year. The Dean always chaired the meetings. The agendas for the meetings were prepared in advance and distributed to all attendees so that they would be prepared to discuss the relevant topics.

As these cordial meetings began, each of the topics was addressed and each of the faculty members was encouraged to participate fully. Most of the topics were thoroughly discussed and appropriate actions items were assigned by the Dean to ensure progress; closure would be made on a timely basis.

The faculty members were very qualified to teach the courses that were assigned to them, and many had achieved tenure with the university; that in itself was an accomplishment. Acquiring tenure required a great deal of time for research and the related writing to prepare for publication, and this was very time-consuming. When this occurred, which it did for many, this took time away from preparation of their lectures in the classroom. Maintaining the scheduled office hours was also not treated with the importance it deserved. This, too, was an opportunity to ensure that each of the students could depend on these faculty members if needed.

It is my very strong view that this is not fair to the students. This type of teaching behavior should never be allowed to exist. All students deserve and need an environment that gives them the opportunity to learn. Learning involves having a teacher who is totally committed to understanding their needs. The committed teacher establishes an environment in the classroom and during office hours whereby all students look forward to each of the scheduled lectures because they know they will learn something new.

In the classroom, there is nothing more important than ensuring that students' learning experiences are as positive and complete as possible. The imparting of useful and realistic knowledge should be the highest priority for all faculty members.

In the university being described, it was often observed that the students were not getting the quality lectures they were expecting. This was supported by a certain percentage of students expressing concern.

Lessons

The learning process is one of the most complex topics of the scholarly world. This case clearly supports the need for faculty members to become more committed to the students they are responsible to teach. All students deserve the very best that each faculty member is able to give them. In many ways, the teacher is a role model, mentor, and friend. Teachers provide the leadership in the classroom.

The student comes first

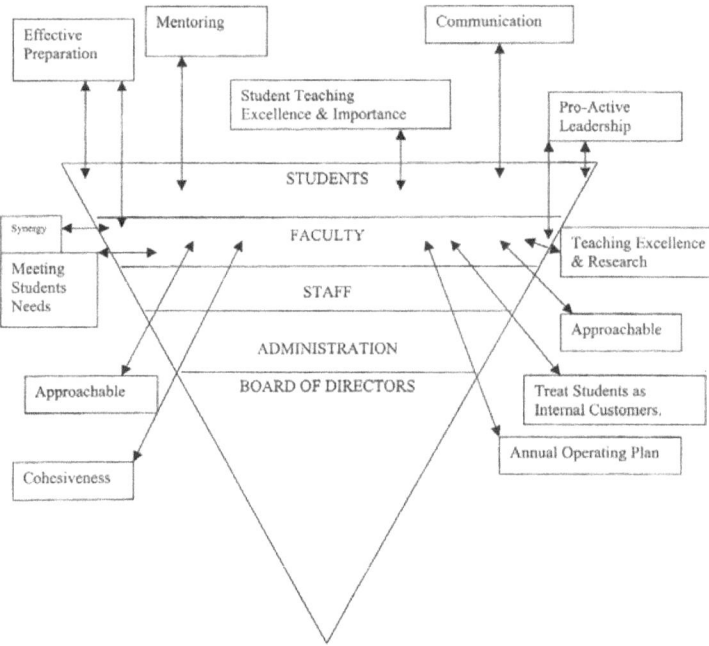

Figure H

Case Study I

NEW HOTEL OPENING – LACK OF LEADERSHIP

After the construction of a new hotel is completed, there are many plans that need to be implemented for a timely and successful opening.

Typically, the plans begin at the corporate office and are then implemented by a team of experienced hotel professionals. The team of professionals holds the key positions for each of the disciplines—human resources, food and beverage, housekeeping, rooms, marketing, finance, and engineering.

This case study describes a major hotel corporation that had built a new hotel in a major city, and had scheduled a date for the grand opening. Prior to this, as an important part of the planning process, the furniture, bedding, kitchen equipment, food, and other items were purchased in preparation for a "soft opening." The purpose of the soft opening is to get the "bugs" out of the systems before welcoming guests. Another important part of the planning was the interviewing, hiring, orientation, and training of new employees.

In this particular case, the corporate Human Resources individual did not hold daily meetings with key management members, and this resulted in confusion and uncertainty. Motivation and morale declined, and the scheduled soft opening and grand opening dates were missed. When these dates were missed, more money was needed to support the continuing cost of the opening.

Lessons

This case study illustrates a clear lack of leadership by the corporate Human Resources person. The opening of a new hotel requires continuous communication, hard work, long hours, and sacrifices of all the employees involved to inspire its success.

This case clearly supports the need for strong, proactive leadership for all the strategic goals to to be met. There's no room for politics and incompetence—only leadership—if the organization is to be successful. For this hotel opening, there was a significant need for more meetings—probably daily, in this case—to make sure that all the important objectives were on track to be met. Without effective and useful communication, there is no leadership. This case clearly supports the need for quality communication by leaders.

Case Study J

CRUISE SHIP COMPANY – SUCCESSFUL LEADERSHIP

This case is associated with a very well-known cruise ship company and one of its key managers. This manager's scope of responsibility was the on-board spa and hair salon. This is a very active and popular department for passengers when the ship is underway. This department generates a significant amount of revenue every day for massages, hairstyling, manicures, and so on.

When interviewed, this manager stated that, "providing leadership on a cruise ship can be very intense; you also play a mother figure." Quite often, the staff who report to her become homesick. "So I have to come in and offer my support as their manager," she continued.

With regard to leadership, she said, "We are on a never-ending journey of discovery; we must embrace new knowledge daily to motivate the staff and build strong teams."

She went on describe many aspects of the culture on a cruise ship. The culture on a cruise ship is unique, therefore the leadership must be unique. Managers must be trained, with the added challenge that they are from different countries and cultures. The training is scheduled and takes place frequently to include topics like team building.

Because the morale of the staff is very important, meetings are conducted weekly, and include passenger relations. These meetings include ice breakers that help the diverse crew members to feel more comfortable during the meetings. The manager emphasized the importance of communicating with all her staff using an "open-door policy" to ensure they had access to her as often as they needed to. Her first priority was a one-on-one approach, and to be available at all times to help her people. She stated that building trust among her staff was critically important in order to have a strong team, and to ensure that the department ran smoothly.

This manager's job involved a lot of coaching and counseling to keep her staff motivated, and she also used daily praise. She felt that maintaining a positive attitude was important for being a role model and a mentor. This type of leadership encouraged her staff to use the open-door policy to freely express themselves. She concluded by saying, "Then hitting a wall, we don't turn around and give up, we figure out how to climb it, or work around it."

Lessons

This manager was successful because she put into practice many of the principles of good leadership; weekly meetings that included team bonding, use of an open-door policy and practice, good communication practices, and one-on-one trust relationships with each of her team members.

Case Study K

WHALE-WATCHING TOURIST BOAT

This case study illustrates the importance of leadership and working together for the crew of a whale-watching tourist boat in Alaska. Through the ups and downs of the job, they always referred back to the main characteristics in a boss/leader that always boosted their morale, work ethic, and mood, and provided positivity and the overall enjoyment of their daily work responsibilities.

The crew talked about the following areas that had a positive impact on their working environment.

- Encouragement
- Humility
- Patience
- Positive attitude
- Hard work
- Camaraderie

In their opinion, encouragement produces a craving to work hard. Humility creates an atmosphere in which team work becomes second nature. The crew members went on to say that the lack of these characteristics shows a boss with an ego, with the effect of hindering growth, and a good work ethic.

Why patience? A boss with patience prevents employees from becoming overwhelmed or stressed when performing their jobs. Patience can be a motivator to help employees to perform much better, and can improve morale.

Why a positive attitude? The total vibe of the workplace changes with a positive attitude, which causes the workers to enjoy the work.

Why hard working? I have experienced a boss who wasn't hardworking at all. She didn't go the extra mile. She often complained and only did what she had to do. This created an atmosphere of negativity and a feeling of unfairness. The crew went on to comment, "Who would want to work harder if your boss was setting such a negative example?"

Camaraderie and teamwork? When a team is working well together, it boosts everyone's morale! "We work hard every day performing our duties as deck hands after the tourists leave the boat. We honestly don't think any of us could do it without having a 'team member' mind-set. Work is a blast if you're a team, no matter what you're doing."

The crew members went on to say what they look for in a boss. The boss should look for the good in people. The boss should respect them and encourage them. "This is what our captain does very often. He has the best crew. We have confidence and love working hard for him. He treats his crew amazingly well, and we respect him for this. When we make a mistake, we openly admit it without fear because he is very approachable and a genuine person. He thanks us daily for our efforts and for being the crew on his boat. Now that is a great boss!"

Lessons

Great leadership makes for happy teams. This leader amply demonstrated the importance of encouraging and praising his team. This leadership produced a cohesive team that had fun together, which in turn, produced a great customer experience.

Additional Diagrams and Models

Employment Interview Steps Diagram

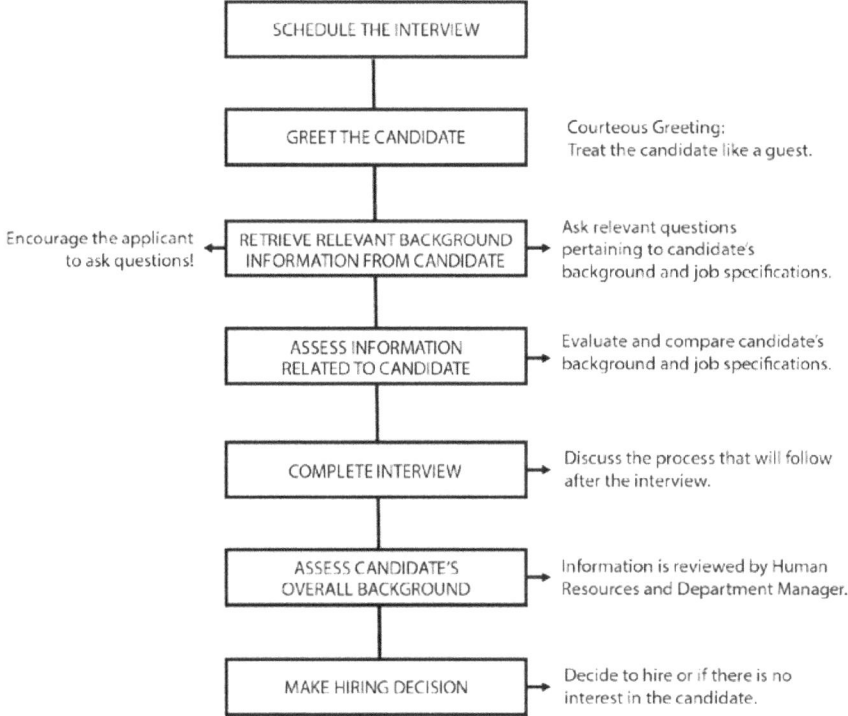

Professional Interview Process Overview

Encourage the applicant to ask questions!

Ask relevant questions pertaining to the candidate's background and job specifications.

Evaluate and compare the candidate's background and and the job specifications.

Describe the process that will follow after the interview.

Review the information with Human Resources and the Department Manager.

Decide whether to hire, or whether there is no interest in the candidate.

Professional Interview Process Model

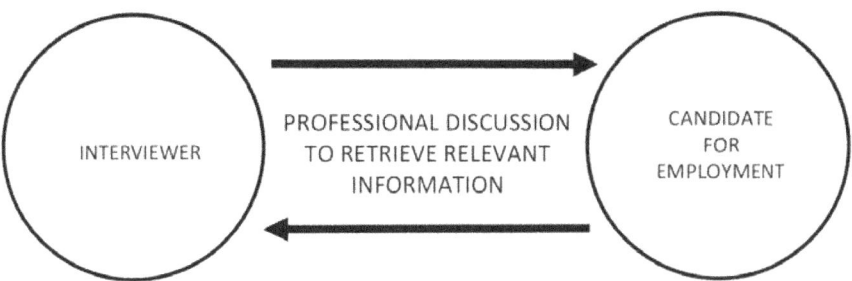

The interview process should NOT be an interrogation!

Each candidate should be treated as a guest of the organization.

Brainstorming Activity Sheet

Fill in the space after each statement.

I am "most talented" when I am:

_____

_____

I am "most likely to succeed" when I am:

_____

_____

I am "most versatile" when I am:

_____

_____

I am "best looking" when I am:

_____

_____

I am "class clown" when I am:

_____

_____

I am "best dressed" when I am:

_____

_____

I am "best dancer" when I am:

_____

_____

I am "most friendly" when I am:
　I am my "best self" when I am:

_____

_____

Worksheet accredited to Dr. Alex Osborn

Notes/Goals

Please use this page to record any ideas, thoughts, future goals, inspirations, and so on, that come to mind while reading through *On the Shoulders of Leaders*.

_____

_____

_____

_____

_____

_____

_____

_____

_____

_____

_____

_____

_____

_____

_____

_____

_____

_____

_____

_____

_____

_____

_____

_____

_____

_____

_____

_____

Author's Personal Note

God is Watching Over Me

With regard to my faith in God, I know that He is always watching over me. I know that He will carry me through many of my life's challenges and disappointments. There is always significant peace in knowing that He has a plan for my life as one of His children.

As the sun rises each day, God gives us a new beginning to enjoy and cherish all of His blessings. I will go forward with my life's journey to find peace within myself through Him, and to enjoy every moment that He has blessed me with.

My faith will continue to be a promise of hope and a path between my heart and God's.

I will always try to remember that I am one of God's children, and His love for me will always be a part of my heart. He is never far away. God is always watching over me.

> Wisdom is precious – PROVERBS 3:13: Happy is the man that findeth wisdom, and the man that getteth understanding. (King James Version)

www.ingramcontent.com/pod-product-compliance
Lightning Source LLC
Chambersburg PA
CBHW051210120626
46547CB00013B/1293